STEM CAREERS
METEOROLOGIST
by Karen Latchana Kenney

pogo

Ideas for Parents and Teachers

Pogo Books let children practice reading informational text while introducing them to nonfiction features such as headings, labels, sidebars, maps, and diagrams, as well as a table of contents, glossary, and index.

Carefully leveled text with a strong photo match offers early fluent readers the support they need to succeed.

Before Reading

- "Walk" through the book and point out the various nonfiction features. Ask the student what purpose each feature serves.
- Look at the glossary together. Read and discuss the words.

Read the Book

- Have the child read the book independently.
- Invite him or her to list questions that arise from reading.

After Reading

- Discuss the child's questions. Talk about how he or she might find answers to those questions.
- Prompt the child to think more. Ask: Do you know anyone who works as a meteorologist? What projects has he or she been involved in? Do you have any interest in this kind of work?

Pogo Books are published by Jump!
5357 Penn Avenue South
Minneapolis, MN 55419
www.jumplibrary.com

Copyright © 2019 Jump!
International copyright reserved in all countries.
No part of this book may be reproduced in any form without written permission from the publisher.

Library of Congress Cataloging-in-Publication Data

Names: Kenney, Karen Latchana, author.
Title: Meteorologist / by Karen Latchana Kenney.
Description: Minneapolis, MN: Jump!, Inc., [2019]
Series: STEM careers | "Pogo Books are published by Jump!" | Audience: Ages 7-10. | Includes index.
Identifiers: LCCN 2018020108 (print)
LCCN 2018025130 (ebook)
ISBN 9781641281898 (ebook)
ISBN 9781641281881 (hardcover: alk. paper)
Subjects: LCSH: Meteorologists–Juvenile literature.
Meteorology–Vocational guidance–Juvenile literature.
Classification: LCC QC869.5 (ebook) | LCC QC869.5
.K46 2019 (print) | DDC 551.5/023–dc23
LC record available at https://lccn.loc.gov/2018020108

Editors: Jenna Trnka and Susanne Bushman
Designer: Michelle Sonnek

Photo Credits: cretolamna/Shutterstock, cover (tablet); SpiffyJ/iStock, cover (weather map); Tomas Ragina/Shutterstock, cover (thermometer); Woody Alec/Shutterstock, cover (barometer); Samuel Borges Photography/Shutterstock, 1 (meteorologist); Pilvitus/Shutterstock, 1 (weather map); Veronica Louro/Shutterstock, 3; Lesleyanne Ryan/Shutterstock, 4; Andrey_Popov/Shutterstock, 5 (meteorologist), 19; Louise Murray/Age Fotostock, 5 (weather map); studio23/Shutterstock, 6-7; David Hay Jones/Science Source, 8; NASA, 9; Fineart1/Shutterstock, 10-11; age fotostock/Alamy, 12-13; Tashi-Delek/iStock, 14-15 (meteorologist); Chuck Eckert/Alamy, 14-15 (weather map); David R. Frazier Photolibrary, Inc./Alamy, 16-17; sirikorn thamniyom/Shutterstock, 18 (child); ojal/Shutterstock, 18 (weather forecast); s_oleg/Shutterstock, 20-21; Brocreative/Shutterstock, 23.

Printed in the United States of America at Corporate Graphics in North Mankato, Minnesota.

TABLE OF CONTENTS

CHAPTER 1

WEATHER WATCHERS

It is the middle of the day, but the sky turns dark. Lightning flashes. Suddenly a loud siren wails. We head for shelter. A **tornado** is near!

The siren is a warning. It is the result of meteorologists' work. They watch the **weather**. They let us know when storms are near. They help keep us safe.

Meteorologists are scientists. They study the **atmosphere**. This is a layer of gases that surrounds Earth. See the blue glow?

The sun heats the atmosphere. It moves the gases. This wind makes weather change. Water moves around the planet, too. This creates clouds and different weather.

atmosphere · · · · · ▶

TAKE A LOOK!

Earth's atmosphere has five layers. The troposphere is the layer closest to Earth. This is where almost all weather happens.

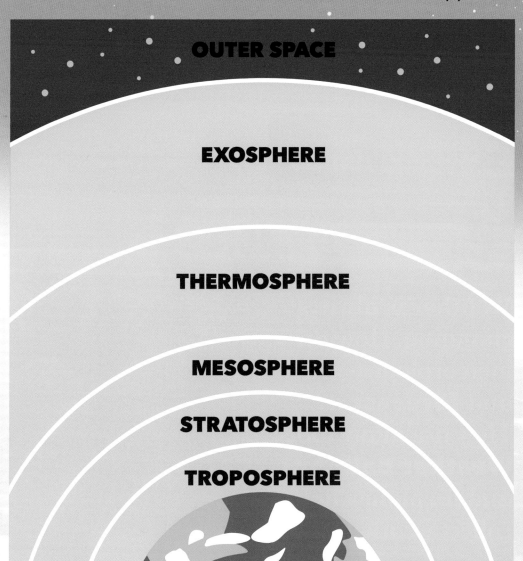

OUTER SPACE

EXOSPHERE

THERMOSPHERE

MESOSPHERE

STRATOSPHERE

TROPOSPHERE

CHAPTER 2

A METEOROLOGIST'S TOOLS

weather
balloon ·····▶

Weather is always changing. How do meteorologists track and **forecast** it? They use many tools. **Weather balloons** and airplanes help collect weather **data**.

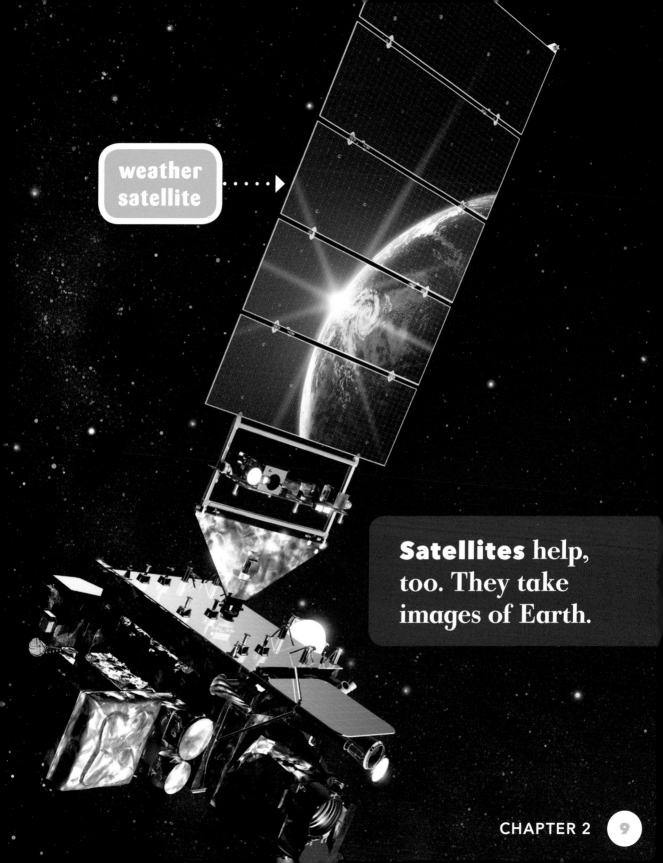

weather
satellite

Satellites help,
too. They take
images of Earth.

Doppler radar towers and **weather stations** help collect data, too. Meteorologists use these tools to follow weather. They track storms. They **predict** future weather.

weather
station

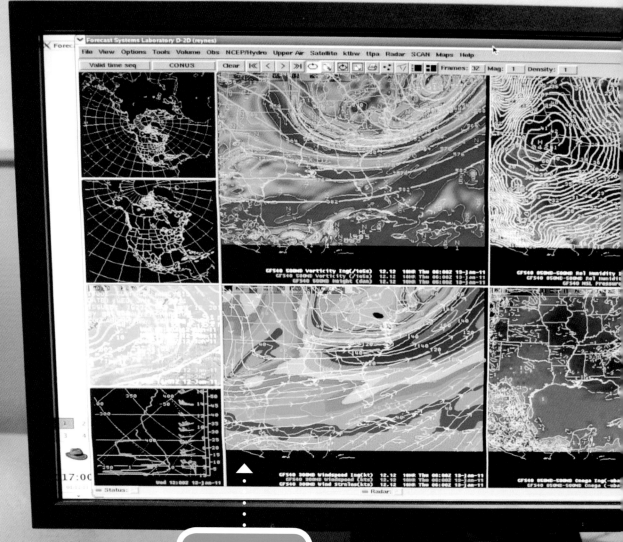

computer
model

This data goes to the National Weather Service. This is a government agency. Meteorologists there analyze the country's weather. They use the data to make **computer models**. These models show how weather might move. They send their forecasts to different parts of the country.

DID YOU KNOW?

When was the first computer model weather prediction made? April 1950. It took more than 24 hours to make.

Some meteorologists work for TV stations. They use the forecasts to predict local and regional weather. They create and show digital maps. They tell TV viewers what weather to expect.

Many have jobs at the National Weather Service. They work at weather stations around the country. Others study severe weather patterns, like **hurricanes**. They also study **air pollution**. Why? To see how it moves in the atmosphere.

Other meteorologists work for companies. Many businesses need to know the weather. Like what? Airports. Why do you think airports need to know about the weather?

DID YOU KNOW?

Baseball teams hire meteorologists. Why? Nice weather means they can play outside games. The military hires them, too. They track weather for missions around the world.

CHAPTER 3

BECOME ONE!

Do you want to track weather? Would you like to help people stay safe? You can be a meteorologist!

Work hard in your science and math classes. Learn as much as you can about computers. And start thinking like a scientist. Be curious about nature. Find the answers to your questions. After high school, you'll need a college degree. You may need a higher degree, too.

As a meteorologist, you can help every day. How? You can help people prepare for bad weather. You can help farmers know when to plant **crops**. You can teach people about keeping our atmosphere healthy. And you can help save lives.

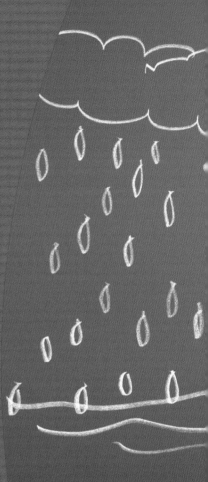

DID YOU KNOW?

To work as a meteorologist, you need STEM skills. What does STEM stand for? Science. Technology. Engineering. Math. STEM careers are in demand. They pay well, too.

ACTIVITIES & TOOLS

TRY THIS!

MOVING AIR

Thunderstorms happen when warm and cold air meet. See how colored water moves just like air in this activity.

What You Need:
- clear, rectangle-shaped container
- water
- measuring cup
- ice cube tray
- blue and red food coloring

1. Pour water in the measuring cup. Add two to three drops of blue food coloring. Pour the blue water into the ice cube tray. Freeze for a few hours until the cubes are solid.

2. Fill the container with warm water. Add two to three drops of red food coloring at one end of the container.

3. Drop a few blue ice cubes in the opposite end of the container.

4. Watch what happens to the blue and red water. Which color rises to the top? Which color sinks to the bottom?

GLOSSARY

air pollution: Chemicals and other harmful substances in the air.

atmosphere: The layer of gases that surrounds Earth and some other planets.

computer models: Representations of real-world systems or processes done on a computer to help calculate and predict.

crops: Plants grown for food or feed for animals.

data: Facts about something.

Doppler radar: A weather tracking system that meteorologists use to find where storms are and how fast they move.

forecast: To calculate or predict.

hurricanes: Large columns of rotating air that form over water.

predict: To make an informed guess about future events based on observation.

satellites: Machines that are sent into space to circle Earth, the moon, the sun, or another planet.

tornado: A large column of rotating air that forms over land.

weather: The conditions in the atmosphere at a particular time and place; weather can be hot or cold, wet or dry, calm or stormy, clear or cloudy.

weather balloons: Large, helium-filled balloons that carry scientific instruments and are released into the sky to gather weather data.

weather stations: Land or sea stations that have instruments to collect weather data.

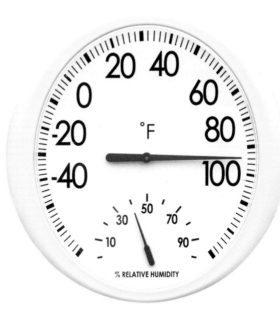

INDEX

TO LEARN MORE

Finding more information is as easy as 1, 2, 3.

1 Go to www.factsurfer.com

2 Enter "meteorologist" into the search box.

3 Click the "Surf" button to see a list of websites.

FACT SURFER